## About the author

Bishop Dr. David Oronsaye is a prophet to the Nations, a seasoned preacher with a mandate to stir up the body of Christ for the end time move of God. He functions powerfully in the prophetic, with signs and wonders following.

A true evangelist driven with a strong passion for the lost, he is also an author of several inspirational books.

He is the co-founder and general overseer of the All Nations Christian Centre international headquarters in London, England.

He is married to Rev. Judith Oronsaye and they are blessed with four daughters.

All Nations Christian Centre
15 York Hill, West Norwood,
London, SE27 0BU
E-mail: drdavid.ancc@gmail.com
Tel: +44 (0)20 8670 0300

Website: www.anccministries.org

# Dedication

I dedicate this book to my
Inspirer,
Leader
and Teacher:
the Holy Spirit.

Adding
knowledge
leads
to
correction

Changed to Change

# The Power of Correction

Bishop Dr. David Oronsaye

Published in the United Kingdom by
Filament Publishing Ltd
16 Croydon Road, Waddon, Croydon,
Surrey, CR0 4PA, United Kingdom
+44(0)20 8688 2598
www.filamentpublishing.com

© 2015 Bishop Dr. David Oronsaye

ISBN 978-1-910125-90-8

Printed by IngramSpark

The right of Bishop Dr. David Oronsaye to be identified as the author of this work has been asserted by him in accordance with the Designs and Copyright Act 1988.

This book is subject to international copyright and may not be copied in any way without the prior written permission of the publishers.

All Scripture quotations are from the New International Version of the Bible, except otherwise stated.

# TABLE OF CONTENTS

| | | |
|---|---|---|
| INTRODUCTION | | 9 |
| CHAPTER ONE | Correction Skills | 13 |
| CHAPTER TWO | Strengthen your brethren | 20 |
| CHAPTER THREE | Effects of Correction | 25 |
| CHAPTER FOUR | Alignment with Exact Destiny | 32 |
| CHAPTER FIVE | Know God as God | 35 |
| CHAPTER SIX | Fear the Lord | 45 |
| CHAPTER SEVEN | Keep Watching | 52 |
| CHAPTER EIGHT | The Power of Change | 57 |
| APPENDIX | | 59 |

When change occurs, there is always a difference by way of action or character

# INTRODUCTION

Jeremiah 10:23-24  Jeremiah's Prayer
*$^{23}$ I know, Lord, that our lives are not our own.*
*We are not able to plan our own course.*
*$^{24}$ So correct me, Lord, but please be gentle.*
*Do not correct me in anger, for I would die.*

To change connotes something or someone becoming different from what it once was. It means reformation, rearrangement and having a different shape, character, form, behaviour and perspective to the former. In Jeremiah 11:6-9, we read:

*$^6$ Then the Lord said, "Broadcast this message in the streets of Jerusalem. Go from town to town throughout the land and say, 'Remember the ancient covenant, and do everything it requires. $^7$ For I solemnly warned your ancestors when I brought them out of Egypt, "Obey me!" I have repeated this warning over and over to this day, $^8$ but your ancestors did not listen or even pay attention. Instead, they stubbornly followed their own evil desires. And because they refused to obey, I brought upon them all the curses described in this covenant.*

Whenever a positive change takes place, it means that the former is no longer useful or desirable; it is out of place, outdated, unpleasant and in need of replacement.

The topic of change is one which men frequently talk about. They desire to apply some kind of transformation into their life, business and day-to-day activities but experience little result.

Today's society is known as the "microwave generation". People expect things instantly: fame, recognition, success – you name it, and someone will be able to offer you direction to the quickest route. With the trend of things being the way they are these days, there has become a potent need for change in every area of life. Without change, our lives remain stagnant. Everything remains in a dormant form or position until change comes, and successful change must be carried out step-by-step: one action and one decision at a time.

Change, by its nature, never allows anything to remain in its former state. When change occurs, there is always a difference by way of action or character. The process of change does not just happen. It comes through the power of correction, that is, when a situation has become obsolete and archaic.

Examples can be deduced in a country where a state or borough is being created and allocations granted. Changes will begin to take place in the environment and in the welfare of the populace. You will notice that everything will begin to change shape and the quality of life for those living in the area will improve. New businesses will begin to spring up in every corner, and good roads and amenities will be provided to effect a change.

In this vein, it will be seen that because of such external changes the life of the people will change. That means the change in the environment becomes a way of changing the people.

It is when things are corrected that change occurs. We shall discuss how correction can change a man and when he is changed, the need for him to change another, a process I refer to as impact. May there be an all round change in your life after reading this book. I pray that your life will be transformed, that alterations and adjustments that advance your life and refine your character will be made. I know that this book will teach you, correct you and align you with your real destiny in Christ.

~

Change and correction are interwoven; correction is the urge to change for the better

# CHAPTER ONE

# CORRECTION SKILLS

Correction is the process of amendment or improvement to a person or situation. It is putting right what was wrong, the act of correcting the mistakes already done. Correction is the ability to lay aside what you believe is right, for what is truly right. This is the exchange of error for truth.

Prov. 29:1: *Whoever stubbornly refuses to accept criticism will suddenly be destroyed beyond recovery.*

It is the action of changing imperfection to perfection. It is a shift from incorrectness to the state of correctness. It is correcting a situation for an acceptable state. It is to rectify an error and bring out the truth. Correction is the cancellation of wrong action for right action. It is the pulling down of the power of errors, mistakes, wrong choices, poor attitudes and behaviour, misunderstanding, ignorance, immaturity and misinformation. The Bible points it to us in 1 Cor. 5:17 that when we have accepted Christ, we become a new creature, and old things shall pass away. That is putting right what was damaged. And 2 Tim. 3:16 also tells us that the Bible was written to correct us:

*¹⁶ All Scripture is inspired by God and is useful to teach us what is true and to make us realise what is wrong in our lives. It corrects us when we are wrong and teaches us to do what is right.*
*¹⁷ God uses it to prepare and equip his people to do every good work.*

This means that God wants us to live and be corrected and change. Deut. 4:36 says:

*Out of heaven, he made you to hear his voice, that he might instruct you, and upon earth, he showed you his great fire, and you heard his words out of the midst of the fire.*

Many received their instructions out of the midst of great fire. God causes us to hear His voice. He instructs us in the way that we should go. When this is done, He then corrects us and changes our lives into what He desires and thus empowers us to be able to impart wisdom and correction to others around us.

Change and correction are interwoven; correction is the urge to change for the better. Before anyone could be referred to as a changed person, he must have been on the other side of life. The side that did not glorify and honour God, nor bring profit to God or mankind. The Word of God says in Isaiah 43:18-19:

*Remember you not the former things, neither consider the things of old. Behold, I will do a new thing, now it shall spring forth, shall you not know it? I will even make a way in the wilderness and rivers in the desert*

When God corrects a man through His Word, He causes him to forget about his origin, background, skills, call or anything else, because He will take over your life and make all things new. Consequently, you no longer live on your own, but according to God's leadership. He speaks out of heaven to His people who are His own. There is no man who obeys the voice of correction and remains the same. Once changed, a generation is changed forever, because there shall be great impartation, for it is written, a seed shall become a generation.

A well corrected and behaved seed will transfer the knowledge to his seed, thus an entire generation is often affected.

Correction is an empowerment to the way of adequate preparation for excellence and better performance. It is a scale for promotion and a ladder of acceptance to a specific assignment. He that refuses correction becomes a tool which the enemies can operate through. Many in the body of Christ have lost the sense of following; they become distracted, frustrated, self-governed and unaccountable because they ignore correction.

He that refuses correction is an enemy of progress, a satanic agent and a hindrance to expansion, development and excellence. Such also is a catalyst of confusion and total darkness. The readiness to receive correction promotes order and brings light.

Genesis 1:1-3 says: *In the beginning, God created the heaven and the earth. The earth was without form and void, and darkness was upon the face of the deep. And the spirit of God moved upon the face of the waters.*

John 1:5 says: *"And the light shines in darkness and the darkness comprehended it not."* The acceptance to be corrected carries the power of light. Indeed, it is light that pushes away errors. An uncorrected person is a catalyst of disorder and destruction, because he does not feel people's pain, but increases and adds to it. He does not protect, but opens wide all gates and doors for attackers. May this never be your portion in Jesus' name!

Every good child of God must be able to take correction. A corrected person helps to fight the enemies of Christ. He that refuses correction never discloses vital information for the enhancement of his organisation. He that refuses correction initiates unrest and crisis. 1 John 4:4-6 says:

[4] *But you belong to God, my dear children. You have already won a victory over those people, because the Spirit who lives in you is greater than the spirit who lives in the world.* [5] *Those people belong to this world, so they speak from the world's viewpoint, and the world listens to them.*
[6] *But we belong to God, and those who know God listen to us. If they do not belong to God, they do not listen to us. That is how we know if someone has the Spirit of truth or the spirit of deception.*

Peter responded positively to the correction from our Lord Jesus Christ, by which he was promoted in life. Every form of stagnancy that was holding his destiny left him. On several occasions, Jesus Christ corrected Peter, yet he did not refuse the correction. One of such occasion was when Jesus was walking on water:

*And immediately Jesus stretched forth his hand and caught him and said unto him, you of little faith, wherefore did you doubt?*

In Matthew 26:40: *And he came unto his disciples, and found them asleep, and said unto Peter, what, could you not watch with me one hour?"*

John 21:15-17: *So when they had dined, Jesus said to Simon Peter, Simon, Son of Jonas, Do you love me, He said feed my lambs. He said to him again the second time, Simon, Son of Jonas, Do you love me? He said unto him, yes, Lord you know that I love you, he said, unto him feed my sheep.*

Luke 22: 31-32: *And the Lord said Simon, Simon, behold Satan had desired to have you, that he may sift you as wheat. But I have prayed for you, that your faith fails not, and when you are converted, strengthen your brethren.*

God corrects the son He loves, for who the Lord loves He chastens and scourges every son whom He receives. If we receive correction, promotion follows.

All the previous scriptures were the corrections that Christ gave Peter that made him a pillar of the early church. He was told that upon his revelation of Jesus Christ as the Messiah, the Son of God, shall Jesus builds His Church and the gates of hell shall not prevail against it.

Corrections reorder a man's life and give him a greater destiny. Your success in life will depend on how well you take to corrections. Any man who accepts correction and change will be a blessing to his generation.

Living a Christian life is all about correction and obedience to correction.

The Bible teaches us that we were in the dark before we knew God and suddenly as we came to know Christ, the light of the Lord enveloped us and the former darkness disappeared and we became new. That is why it is instructed that believers should not be unequally yoked with unbelievers in any form, because darkness and light have nothing in common.

A once changed man is not permitted to go back, because it is dangerous and destructive. Your change comes about so that you can aid in the change of another.

Once you have put your hand on the plough, you should not look back, for if you do, you are not fit for the Kingdom of God and all its inheritance. Many people blame God for their afflictions and backwardness, without reflecting that they refuse to adhere to God's corrections. The book of Proverbs talks about a way which seems right to a man, but which ends in death.

Correction from the Lord will cause you to change and make you a channel of blessing to others. Let us see Deuteronomy 28:26:

*And it shall come to pass, if you shall hearken diligently unto the voice of the Lord your God, to observe and to do all his commandments which I command you this day that the Lord God will set you on high above all nations of the earth."*

This is what accepting correction can do. It brings promotion and increase. Anyone who listens to correction and obeys will grow forever. Correction is the watchword to change and your change will benefit others.

∽

# CHAPTER TWO

# STRENGTHEN YOUR BRETHREN

When a man has not first been strengthened, he cannot strengthen others. It takes strength to strengthen others. It takes iron to sharpen iron, wood cannot sharpen iron. So it is with a child of God who has been corrected and strengthened in the inner man, he will be able to strengthen another with boldness through the Word of God. Luke 22:32 says, *But I have prayed for you, that your faith fails not, and when you are converted, strengthen your brethren.*

When you are corrected, changed and are converted, then strengthen your brethren in love, in encouragement, through the Word of God, through gifts, sharing, giving and doing good, wherever you possibly can. Put all efforts to see that the Kingdom of God is populated while the kingdom of darkness is depopulated.

This is the great aim of God concerning us in life. All He wants is that once we are changed, we should be able to change others and not leave them the way they are. You must be able to leave a legacy behind wherever the sole of your feet treads on this earth. He said you shall possess the land. No one possesses land without first having been corrected from above.

One can never give out what is not already within. You will never be able to give what you don't have; it is only what you possess that you can give out. A blind man cannot lead the blind, lest the two fall.

Paul met with the Lord on his way to destroy the children of God in Damascus. After his encounter, a great change came and he was transformed from a destroyer of good things to a builder in the Body of Christ and a converter of many Gentiles to Christ and His Kingdom. Just because of the change he encountered, he became a pillar of change to the Body of Christ. He had a testimony that he had run the race and finished the course. He fought against unbelief and said 'I have fought the good fight of faith.'

Many people knew him to be a murderer, but when change came, it became a different story entirely. That is the evidence of change in people's lives. He was able to strengthen everyone he met along his way through the strength of God he received on the day of his change.

Nobody will receive correction and remain unfruitful. Fruitfulness comes by change in correction. Once you are changed, you cannot afford to keep quiet because His Word will be like fire in your bones, which you will find impossible to retain on the inside.

You will find out that you involuntarily go about telling people of the goodness of God. A testimony will always give you another testimony.

Why do men and women of God love to correct people through the Word of God? It is because they have listened to the corrections of the Word and they accepted it, applied it and then they saw it worked for them. Now, by the effects of the Word, they are transformed and are then able to play a role in the transformation of others.

My life today would not have been what it is if it were not that somebody who was changed by the Word of God located me and caused me to change also by introducing me to Christ and His good works. Today, I am a living witness of what change can bring about in a person's life.

No one who has been changed by God's correction can go astray. Your life can never remain the same if you are truly changed. A lit candle will always light up another one. You can find out that one lit candle can produce innumerable numbers of lit candles. Therefore it becomes expedient, that once a life is changed, it is also expected to change others, without apology.

When a place is dark and light appears there, it brightens up the area and this righteousness can never be for one person but for everyone who is around it. This is because light attracts.

The amount of glorious things happening around you depends on the amount of light you have through the Word of the God.

So, for you to command results in what you do, you should be able to show forth the light of your changed life to the world around you in order for that world to change also.

No person can be everywhere at the same time, but you can affect a life that will go to where you cannot be able to get to once that person is changed through correction and the truth you reveal to him. Wherever he goes, he will also bring correction and change to the people he meets on his way, and on and on - as your change continues to progress from glory to glory.

One thing with a changed life is that you can never remain where the change met you. Change will most definitely take you to a higher place once you accept correction.

Accepting correction from the Word of God is the beginning of wisdom. Once you accept, it means you are blessed, for the Bible informs us that blessed is everyone who trembles at the Word of God. Job 5:17 says: *Behold, happy is the man whom God corrects, therefore despise not the chastening of the Almighty.*

Anyone who allows the Word of God to correct and control his life shall ever be happy. Once God corrects you, take it with all your heart for who God loves, He corrects.

Every man's greatness depends on the amount of correction he receives from God.

No one who is born of God, created by God whose life is in the hand of God, is permitted to despise the corrections of God. Jesus in John 10:10 declares: *I have come that they might have life and have it more abundantly.* Once you accept corrections, you immediately begin to receive abundant life, promotion and increase in all realms of your existence.

Those who knew you before will begin to call you blessed of the Lord, because old things in you must have passed away and all things would have become new in your life. This newness will in turn make people come to the light of your change. But a nation, man or woman who does not accept correction from God can never be fruitful in life. Psalm 50:17 says: *Seeing that you hate instruction and cast my word behind you.* If you refuse to listen to God's instruction and fail to hide His Word behind you, there shall be no fruitfulness. This is because what you don't have, you cannot give to anyone. Today, if you have received this instruction, pass it over to someone else and see transformation.

# CHAPTER THREE

# EFFECTS OF CORRECTION

*And the Gentiles shall come to our light, and kings to the brightness of your rising.* (Isaiah 60:3)

A well corrected life that is in readiness to accept whatsoever the Lord speaks to him will forever be on the rising track. Now on your rising, so many good things will begin to take place all around you because the people who did not know you before, will begin to know you, and the people who never knew God nor believed in His existence, will begin to come to your light. Kings which would have been difficult for you to locate and meet will on their own accord come to the brightness of your rising.

The only thing God demands from you is to be corrected. Once this is done, every other thing shall be added. You do not need to seek for connections anymore because the correction you have already received will make way for you and you will begin to find yourself at the right place, at the right time, with the right people. Heeding to correction will open doors of blessings, fame and glory by which men will know you and come over in celebration of your Source of Greatness.

God Himself cannot come down to do things for Himself; that is why He created you in His own image and likeness and made you a channel by which He can reach the world, if you embrace correction. Leadership is arrived at through a process of correction. People choose leaders once they see that a person's life is an example to others. People use that life as a light to brighten their own path. A well corrected life is brightness to others. It is like a mirror which others look into, aim to resemble, and remove any stain or blemish in their lives.

I met with a man whose habit was excessive drinking of alcohol and smoking. He had been doing these things for many years. Because I have been corrected through the Word of God, I began to open his eyes to what the Word of God says about sinful habits. He was amazed and, gradually, he renounced and overcame all those bad habits. Today he is a totally changed man to God's own glory.

Kings shall surely come to the brightness of your rising. You rose so that nations may know God and come to the knowledge of the truth. You did not rise ordinarily. Your rising means glory and increase for the Kingdom of God.

When Jesus came to the earth, something great happened. He came to correct the pride and self-centeredness of humanity, He was humiliated and died.

But He rose and a lot of lives were changed and transformed through Him. He wants you to imitate Him and be the same thing to your world. Multitudes came to the rising of the Son of God and He told us that greater works than these shall we do. If we shall do greater works than He did, we shall need to receive instructions from God Almighty as Jesus did. These instructions will order our lives and steps; for where there is order, there is bound to be rapid progress, perfection and maturity.

No man has ever come to the knowledge of truth in correction and remained the same. It pays to receive correction; your generation will never forget that you came into the world at such a time like this.

Accepting correction is the watchword for progress. Even in a family, a child who accepts correction of his or her father and mother will be loved and blessed above the rest of the children.

In First Corinth. 13:11, Paul says: *When I was a child, I spake as a child, I understood as a child, I thought as a child, but when I became a man, I put away childish things.*

A person that refuses God's instructions will ever remain a child. Know that a son differs not from a slave if he refuses his father's instructions. When Paul was a child, he thought and spoke like a child.

It was when he received corrections that he realised that he could no longer continue in this way because he had to mature in order to bring others also into the maturity of the Word of God.

Arise now, and begin to adhere to instructions that will make you glorious in life. Know that your maturity in the Word of God will make it possible for you to positively affect every life that you come in contact with anywhere on the earth.

If your life is not yet making an impact, you need to arise. It does not matter what you do; no one should despise the days of small beginnings for it shall go from glory to glory until perfection. You are created for impact and corrected for the demonstration of God's power.

Correction prevents us from making repeated mistakes that might destroy lives and organisations, thus causing confusion. This is because correction brings promotion in life. One corrected life will forever rise and shine because of the revelation of the Word on his inside. It is written, "your word have I hid in my heart that I may not sin against you" and "for your word is sharper than a two edged sword." Once the Word of God is hid within a man, his lifestyle begins to show forth the glory of God and this in turn brings men back to God, for they are now able to see the goodness of God in your life.

They will be compelled and motivated to come over to the goodness and glory of God, thereby increasing the Kingdom of God and decreasing the kingdom of darkness forever.

A changed life is a threat to the enemy because he knows that applied knowledge is power, and that he is only able to destroy a person who lacks knowledge and the understanding to apply it.

Therefore, my dear reader, arise above the enemy. Get knowledge in your area of specialisation. But with all your getting, get understanding and this will make your life worth celebrating. Your generation shall then rise to call you blessed.

The correction a man receives is for his benefit and could lead to the liberation of millions of souls. This is because wherever he goes, he impacts people and they which are corrected through him will in turn correct others, and on and on it goes forever.

My blessed reader, it is now time for you to receive correction concerning your life's endeavours. This will make a great nation out of you forever. Know that a seed shall eventually become a generation. Seeds sown into the ground at the right season will surely sprout and produce a bountiful harvest of crops.

When Abraham was called and corrected and commanded to leave his father's house, he wholeheartedly obeyed the instructions.

From the moment of departing from his father's house, he never diminished; rather, he was elevated the more, and his blessings multiplied in all areas.

Today, everyone in the Body of Christ claims the Abrahamic blessings, yet many believers are not willing to take correction in the same way as Abraham did. Any church that preaches much on correction has a lot to contend with as only few people are prepared to identify with the message because of their itching ears that only desire to hear sweet things. Heaven is real and hell is real; you cannot run away from this truth. This is the reason why we must arise unto righteousness through the corrections of God and begin to live our lives in the light of truth, and men - kings, the crème de la crème of every society, will begin to come to the rising of your light according to the Word of God.

Abraham's life was a life of correction which brought about great changes and gains to him and his descendants forever. If he did not agree to God's correction, he would not have been blessed to overflowing the way he was. But glory be to the Lord who delivered grace to Abraham and caused him to be blessed as it is written in Gen. 24:1: *And Abraham was old and well stricken in age and the Lord had blessed Abraham in all things.* He possessed long life, was full of comfort and well stricken in age. He enjoyed life, and overcame unfruitfulness after his correction and became richly blessed in all things.

What else do you want from life if not fulfilment on all sides? Hence you must love and hold on to correction. Abraham is a good example. He was so focused that instead of giving Lot, his cousin, room to distract him, he peacefully called for cordial separation between the two of them.

Hebrew 11: 8-10 says: *By faith Abraham when he was called to go out into a place which he should after received for an inheritance, obeyed and he went out not knowing where he went. By faith, he sojourned in a land of promise, as in a strange country. Dwelling in tabernacles with Isaac and Jacob, the heirs with him of the same promise. For he looked for a city which had foundations, whose builder and maker is God.*

Abraham did this because he recognised that God was his ultimate. This is also what you must do in all areas of your life. Learn to seek first the Kingdom of God and His righteousness, and all other things shall be added unto you. Abraham sought the Kingdom and was richly blessed in all things.

Whoever accepts correction will ever be celebrated in life; therefore correction makes you a celebrity in life. Today as you read this, arise and accept the corrections being given to you, for they shall make your life worth living.

# CHAPTER FOUR

# ALIGNMENT WITH EXACT DESTINY

In this chapter, we shall look at the power of correction and its works upon a man's destiny. Correction prevents disorderliness in life. When a person is being corrected, their life begins to align itself with the real destiny that God ordained.

Before I was corrected by the Word of God, I lived life in my own way and by my own rules. I did not know that it was not the right way but, alas, someone met me with the gospel, corrected me, and I accepted it. It was then I noticed, little by little, that I found myself on route to the destiny I am in today and it is actually working and will continue to work.

Once your life is corrected, you begin to see differences in your life. You will no longer wish to continue in your old ways as you begin to enter into a new realm with God and man. Your level of understanding will begin to surpass what it once was. The willingness to accept correction reveals your true destiny, and your willingness to acknowledge accountability. Once a man is aligned with his real destiny, he makes more impact in the world. This is because correction will open your eyes to the hidden treasures God has kept in store for you.

Many people are stars on earth today but will never know it until they accept correction through the Word of God. The Bible says: *Blessed is everyone who the Lord corrects.* This is a true saying because a corrected person shall surely prosper if he accepts corrections wholeheartedly.

Those who did accept correction went far in life. Just like the case of Saul who was renamed Paul. Saul started on the wrong track. Satan used him against the Kingdom of God; he was diverted and tricked by Satan's lies. Saul persecuted and slaughtered many people in churches everywhere he went. But when Jesus Christ, Himself, corrected him, he took the correction and aligned his destiny to it. He became a mighty instrument in the Kingdom of God and finished his course well. He worked with all tenacity of life and he became a great achiever who made it through perils, trials and tribulations.

After his correction took place, he did not confer with flesh and blood. He moved round with all his heart to bring back beauty into the Kingdom of God which he was once fought against.

What can separate us from the love of God? Nothing at all is permitted to separate us. We should know that in all things we are more than conquerors. We can do all things through Christ that strengthens us.

Once the Word of God corrects you, the Spirit of Christ takes over the direction of your life. Once the Spirit of Christ takes over, He begins to order your destiny into what it was created for and you will no longer go through life with uncertainty. Whoever is in the know, can never be disappointed in life. Knowledge is power as Hosea 4:6 states: *My people are destroyed for lack of knowledge.*

Lack of knowledge of who they are has made a mess out of their lives. They no longer enjoy the glory of God nor know the things that are prepared for their destiny. It was when I received knowledge, through correction in the Word of God, that I began to align myself with what God's Word says. My destiny then arose and blossomed to what it is today, and forever I shall continue to blossom and show forth the glory of God in all areas of my life and destiny.

Anyone who accepts correction will always bring glory to their father and mother. It goes from generation to generation because what you have you can give to your children, and your children will also give to their own children, and on and on it goes forever in Jesus' name.

Anybody who accepts correction can never be a failure in life. No one celebrates a failure because nobody wants to fail. I am a living witness of what I am talking about. Before I came to the knowledge of the truth, I was a failure. It was when the Word of God came to me and I decided to accept correction that I began to see a vast and colourful destiny that God ordained for me to encounter in my lifetime. Hence I decided never to give up in any matter of my destiny until accomplishment. Arise today and begin to accept instruction. This will bring you to a higher place than where you are today.

# CHAPTER FIVE

# KNOW GOD AS GOD

The power of correction enables a man to know God as God. Though before correction he must have come to the realisation that there is a God in heaven, when it comes to how powerful God is, he may lack understanding. However, when he gets converted, he begins to have a better understanding of who God is. God himself will begin to reveal unto him His divine power for the accomplishment of his destiny.

Dan 11:32: *And such as do wickedly against the covenant shall he corrupt by flatteries: but the people that do know their God shall be strong and do exploits.*

It is very important to know God for who He is. This is the reason why a lot of instructions have been written down to that effect in the Bible, so that whoever reads them shall embrace and run with the words to attain salvation and glory. Those who do know their God shall be strong and do exploits. Doing exploits in life is dependent on how much knowledge of God you have. The deeper, the better. Dig deep into God to know who He is, the power He has and all the things He can do for you.

In the course of finding this out, you will get deeper into the knowledge of His power and this will make you a wonder to your world because men around you will see the confidence and boldness by which you operate. This will attract them to your own world and endeavours.

I have never seen any man who truly knows God go astray. This is because He uses His right hand of righteousness to deliver you and set you free forever. Many people on earth today refuse instructions because they do not know Him well. If they did, they would not have delayed or wasted their time on those things that do not profit. Many, who have now passed away, had things in their destinies they left undone, just because they did not know God as God.

Adding knowledge leads to correction.

Hosea 4:6-8:

*⁶ My people are destroyed for lack of knowledge: because thou hast rejected knowledge, I will also reject thee, that thou shalt be no priest to me: seeing thou hast forgotten the law of thy God, I will also forget thy children. ⁷ As they were increased, so they sinned against me: therefore will I change their glory into shame. 8 They eat up the sin of my people, and they set their heart on their iniquity."*

Add to your faith, character, and to character, knowledge:

Do you want to be a good mother? Add knowledge

Do you want to be a good wife or husband? Add knowledge

Do you want to be a good Sunday school teacher? Add knowledge

Do you want to be a good usher? Add knowledge

Do you want to be a good Christian? Add knowledge

Do you want to be a good business man? Add knowledge

Do you want to be a good intercessor? Add knowledge

The word "knowledge" in Greek is the same word for "light". Paul prayed for the eyes of the Colossians' and Ephesians' to be enlightened that they may know what has been freely given. Read Hebrew 6:4 - enlightened people very rarely forget what they have known.

The word "ignorance" in Greek is the same word for "darkness", and Satan is the prince of darkness. The Scripture says the god of this world has blinded their eyes lest they see and repent and turn to God. The only power capable of destroying a Christian scripturally is not Satan, sickness, government, etc. but ignorance. We cannot afford to be ignorant of the devices of the enemy lest Satan takes advantage of us.

John 8:32: *Ye Shall know the Truth and the truth shall set you free.*

What is truth? "Thy Word is truth." Right, there is the solution to most, if not all, of our problems. But how many of us read God's Word or even pay attention to it? But we cry daily for deliverance. Run from one mountain to another, binding and loosing. May the Lord help us to simply heed to His Word that it may go well with us.

The truth is there, to set you free, but you must seek to know the truth.

Knowledge is the light that brings deliverance. If we are content with just being saved and don't add knowledge, we will suffer as Christians.

All Jesus has won for us is available for us through the knowledge of Him. No wonder Paul prayed that I might know Him.

Even in the Scripture of 1 Peter, we are told we receive a multiplication of grace and peace through the knowledge of God and Christ.

Therefore we must position ourselves to seek the knowledge of God and Christ.

In Daniel, we are told, *those who know their God will be strong and do exploit.*

Serving God must be done in knowledge with understanding. Uzzah died in His attempt to serve God by putting his hand where he did not need to. David abandoned God's Ark in perplexity but later came back, having been educated on how to handle it with sacrifice, reverence and worship.

It is not the truth that sets you free but it is the knowledge of truth that sets you free.

Eph 1:18: *The eyes of your understanding being enlightened; that ye may know what is the hope of his calling, and what the riches of the glory of his inheritance in the saints." Heb 6:4: "For it is impossible for those who were once enlightened, and have tasted of the heavenly gift, and were made partakers of the Holy Ghost.*

2 Peter 1:1-End:
*¹ Simon Peter, a servant and an apostle of Jesus Christ, to them that have obtained like precious faith with us through the righteousness of God and our Saviour Jesus Christ: 2 Grace and peace be multiplied unto you through the knowledge of God, and of Jesus our Lord, 3 According as his divine power hath given unto us all things that pertain unto life and godliness, through the knowledge of him that hath called us to glory and virtue:*

*⁴ Whereby are given unto us exceeding great and precious promises: that by these ye might be partakers of the divine nature, having escaped the corruption that is in the world through lust.*

*⁵ And beside this, giving all diligence, add to your faith virtue; and to virtue knowledge; 6 And to knowledge temperance; and to temperance patience; and to patience godliness; ⁷ And to godliness brotherly kindness; and to brotherly kindness charity. ⁸ For if these things be in you, and abound, they make you that ye shall neither be barren nor unfruitful in the knowledge of our Lord Jesus Christ. ⁹ But he that lacketh these things is blind, and cannot see afar off, and hath forgotten that he was purged from his old sins. ¹⁰ Wherefore the rather, brethren, give diligence to make your calling and election sure: for if ye do these things, ye shall never fall: ¹¹ For so an entrance shall be ministered unto you abundantly into the everlasting kingdom of our Lord and Saviour Jesus Christ.*

*¹² Wherefore I will not be negligent to put you always in remembrance of these things, though ye know them, and be established in the present truth. ¹³ Yea, I think it meet, as long as I am in this tabernacle, to stir you up by putting you in remembrance; ¹⁴ Knowing that shortly I must put off this my tabernacle, even as our Lord Jesus Christ hath shewed me. ¹⁵ Moreover I will endeavour that ye may be able after my decease to have these things always in remembrance.*
*¹⁶ For we have not followed cunningly devised fables, when we made known unto you the power and coming of our Lord Jesus Christ, but were eyewitnesses of his majesty. ¹⁷ For he received from God the Father honour and glory, when there came such a voice to him from the excellent glory, This is my beloved Son, in whom I am well pleased. ¹⁸ And this voice which came from*

*heaven we heard, when we were with him in the holy mount.*
*[19] We have also a more sure word of prophecy; whereunto ye do well that ye take heed, as unto a light that shineth in a dark place, until the day dawn, and the day star arise in your hearts: [20] Knowing this first that no prophecy of the scripture is of any private interpretation. 21 For the prophecy came not in old time by the will of man: but holy men of God spake as they were moved by the Holy Ghost.*

Here is the Scripture for promotion in life:
Proverb 4:7-9
*[7] Wisdom is the principal thing; therefore get wisdom: and with all thy getting get understanding. 8 Exalt her, and she shall promote thee: she shall bring thee to honour, when thou dost embrace her. 9 She shall give to thine head an ornament of grace: a crown of glory shall she deliver to thee.*

Wisdom and knowledge can be bought. We spend money on expensive clothes and education, hair, homes, etc. but how much do we spend to acquire knowledge and gain understanding for our promotion in life?

Take correction, reproof and rebuke for success in life. Knowing God fully will make you a success in life. Blessed is everyone who accepts correction from God. Whoever God rebukes is blessed forever. This is because there are many secrets you will be exposed to if you come to God. It is said that the secret things belong to God Almighty.

God says in Jeremiah 1:5: *Before you were formed in your mother's womb, I knew you and before you came out of the womb I sanctified you, and I ordained you a prophet unto the nations.*

If God knew you before you were formed, it means that He knows your make-up, your frame, capability and what you have the capacity to contain in every area of life. It is better to go to this God who knows everything about me so I can gain speed in my life endeavours without the stress of trying to figure it all out myself. Many people suffer on earth today because of stubbornness to receive the correction God is giving. Refusal to take instruction, leads to a difficult and unfulfilled life. This causes a lot of frustration and such a life will never be able to change another.

Everyone is changed to change another person on earth. If you do not actualise your purpose, somewhere, another person may suffer as a result of your failure. Why? Because our destinies are connected. The world is made up of a network of people with joint purposes. We may all have different purposes on earth, but under God's direction, there is unison and harmony.

Know God as God and things will work out well for you. Whoever believes will not perish but have life everlasting. For you not to perish is to know God, and allow His Spirit to continually direct you in all areas of your life endeavours. Nobody who knows God as God will ever suffer loss.

If everyone in the Body of Christ will know God as God, heaven will open for the Body continually and God's name will forever be glorified.

If I had rejected the correction and offer of salvation, it would have been another problem because there is no way I would have known how to write down all these God-given ideas or inspirations for you to read and run with.

To know God is to have great gain in life. God is love and He so loved us, that He gave His only begotten Son that whosoever believes shall not perish but have life everlasting. Knowing God means everlasting life, peace, joy, liberty, freedom, fame and glory.

The joy of salvation will grow, increase and multiply. It leads to an evergreen life which will not wither, but shine brighter day by day.

Psalm 1:1-3 says: *Blessed is the man that walks not in the counsel of the ungodly nor stands in the way of sinners nor sits in the seat of the scornful. But his delight is in the law of the Lord and in his law does he meditate day and night. And he shall be like a tree planted by the rivers of water, that brings forth its fruit in its season, his leaf also shall not wither and whatsoever he does shall prosper.*

This is a man who knows his God. All his cases are settled forever, because his provisions are sure. Water will be supplied to him, strength and greenness become his portion, and nothing shall by any means stunt his growth or stop his development.

Forever and ever all things will work together for good for him in all areas of his life and destiny. Therefore, shun evil, and enjoy the blessing of God. Don't be like many people who look for blessings outside of God's provision. Such people do not believe they are wrong, and so cannot be corrected to change their ways of life. They will regret this at the end of their lives.

∼

# CHAPTER SIX

# FEAR THE LORD

To be corrected means to fear the Lord at all times in all areas of life. By fear, I do not mean that you must be scared of the Lord, as our relationship with the Heavenly Father is one founded on His love for us. To fear God is to honour Him, hold Him in high esteem. It is to reverence Him and count His Word as weighty. There is no one who has ever feared God yet remained stagnant. The Bible says that the fear of the Lord is the beginning of wisdom and wisdom is the principal thing you need to succeed here on earth.

It is wisdom to depart from evil and do good; to allow the Word of God to have dominion over your life and in all things. It is wisdom to always put God first in all things, giving Him every reverence He deserves in order for glory to appear in your life. Fear God and keep to all His commandments. Anything He commands you to do, do it with all your heart and you will see great things happen to you. Those who fear God always tremble at His Word. Once the Word of God is released, they tremble at it and fear and decide to do all that is written on it. These are the ones who fear the Lord and who will be blessed of the Lord.

Isa 66:2: *My hands have made both heaven and earth; they and everything in them are mine. I, the Lord, have spoken! I will bless those who have humble and contrite hearts, who tremble at my word.*

Isa 66:5: *Hear this message from the Lord, all you who tremble at his words: "Your own people hate you and throw you out for being loyal to my name. 'Let the Lord be honoured!' they scoff. 'Be joyful in him!' But they will be put to shame.*

Why did the Word of God say that the righteous man shall be like a tree planted by the rivers of waters? It is just because once you are corrected and you align yourself with godly character, God becomes your all in all. He carries you while you follow along. He is that river that does not run dry. He supplies, on a daily basis, all your needs according to His riches in glory through the knowledge of Christ.

The fear of the Lord brings reward. The Bible says: *Eyes have not seen, ears have not heard neither has it come to the thoughts of any man what God has in store for them that love him.* It is only when you love God that you can fear him.

Before I received correction by His Word, I used to think that I was the one in charge of my life. It was all about my struggles and my own strength to overcome them.

I thought if I could not do something, no one else could do it for me. I did not know that as I looked unto Him, I would be well cared for. It was one day after I had been preached to by someone, I asked the Lord a question that if I follow him what could He do for me.

He vividly said to me: *If you can seek first my Kingdom and righteousness first in all things about your life, every other thing shall be added unto you.* (Matt. 6:33)

When I heard this, I paused and things turned around in my life for good. From that time, I resolved in my heart never to do anything without putting God first. In prayer, morning by morning, God shows us His mercies and it is only through prayer that you are able to communicate with Him and receive solutions to your problems.

Every morning, you wake up and learn to talk with God in prayer before talking to anyone else. In everything, put God first. Teach the same things to your children and grandchildren so that your generation may continue in the things of God. In office, business or whatever you do, make God the leader and first in all. Tell the world around you also to follow suit and things will forever work out well in all areas of your life.

To fear God is to depart from evil. Look for Him with all your heart, spirit and soul. Make Him the Lord of your life and do not hesitate to shun evil.

Below are Scriptures that admonish us to fear God and depart from evil.

Job 28:28: *"nd unto man he said, Behold, the fear of the Lord, that is wisdom; and to depart from evil is understanding.*

Psa. 34:14: *Depart from evil, and do good; seek peace, and pursue it.*

Psa. 37:27: *Depart from evil, and do good; and dwell for evermore.*

Prov. 3:7: *Be not wise in thine own eyes: fear the LORD, and depart from evil.*

Prov. 13:19: *The desire accomplished is sweet to the soul: but it is abomination to fools to depart from evil.*

Prov. 16:6: *By mercy and truth iniquity is purged: and by the fear of the LORD men depart from evil.*

Prov. 16:17: *The highway of the upright is to depart from evil: he that keepeth his way preserveth his soul.*

Separate yourself today from the evil of the day. Do not entangle yourself with it. Take correction and know that it helps to be corrected. Blessed is every man whom God corrects.

This is because once you receive the correction, you will go places and you will never remain the same. The knowledge you receive makes you a channel of blessing to someone else because you cannot contain it all alone without letting another person know the truth.

Give out the truth to people when you have received it. Obtain the truth through the Word of God and use it to change your world at all times.

Proverbs 8:13 says: *The fear of the Lord is to hate evil, pride and arrogance, and the evil way, and the forward mouth, do I hate.*

Proverbs 9:10 says: *The fear of the Lord is the beginning of wisdom and the knowledge of the Holy is understanding.*

Proverbs 10:27 says: *The fear of the Lord prolongs days, but the years of the wicked shall be shortened.*

Proverbs 10:9 says: *He that walks uprightly walks surely, but he that perverts his ways shall be known.*

Proverbs 11:27 says: *He that diligently seeks good procures favour but he that seeks mischief if all come unto him.*

Proverbs 19:16: *He that keeps the commands keeps his own soul, but he that despise his ways.*

Proverbs 20:18: *Every purpose is established by counsel, and with good advice make war.*

Proverbs 28:20: *A faithful man abounds with blessings but he that makes haste to be rich shall not be innocent.*

The fear of the Lord makes you faithful and causes the world around you to turn to your Source of increase and progress.

Every man born on earth today is created to create. God created you in His own image and likeness. God is a creator and this also makes you a creator and a designer because you are made in His own image. As God created you, and has given you the opportunity to receive correction, He also wants you to do the same for others.

Create something good out of your world. Design someone else's life by becoming a living example of what the Lord says. Cause them to know that as they follow the Word, their lives can never remain the same. Whatever correction God gives to you through His Word is not for you alone, but it is also for the world around you.

Remember that every soul that sins will die. This is why you must be ready to give corrections through the Word of the Lord to a dying world.

God honours His Word more than His name because the Word of the Lord is God Himself according to John 1:1: *In the beginning was the word and the word was with God and the word was God.*

The Scripture teach us that the Word became flesh, the Word of God is Christ Himself, the Word of God is also the will of God. So everyone who believes is expected to continue in it and also give it over to someone else. He receives it and gives to another person, and on and on it goes.

∽

# CHAPTER SEVEN

# KEEP WATCHING

Blessed are those servants whom the Lord, when he comes, shall find watching, verily I say unto you that he shall gird himself, and make them to sit down to meat, and will come forth and serve them.

Blessed is that servant whom his Lord when he comes shall find so doing, of a truth I say to you, he will make him ruler over all that he has (Luke 12:47). Hebrews 10:16: *This is the covenant that I will make with them after those days, says the Lord, I will put my laws into their hearts and in their minds will I write them.*

Ephesians 5:8, 16: *For you were sometime darkness, but now are you lifted in the Lord, walk as children of light. Redeeming the time for the days are evil.*

Ephesians 5:18: *Be not drunk with wine, but be filled with the spirit.*

Colossians 4:2: *Continue in prayers and watch in the same with thanksgiving.*

The most valuable currency we have as human beings is time. Redeem the time, be watchful. Do not allow time to pass you by without correcting an error inside you or around you. It is time to arise and flourish in your area of jurisdiction. Keep watching wherever you may find yourself. Life is all about watchfulness.

Be careful for nothing but watch and pray. Watch with thanksgiving. Do not allow life to pass by without you doing all that God wants of you. He wants you to be celebrated, to be great in all ramifications of life. He wants you to be alive and well in the reign of the Kingdom and He wants to use you to propagate His Kingdom here on earth. You cannot afford to stop the move of God in your life.

Blessed are those servants whom the master shall find watching when he comes. To watch in this aspect, means to keep in mind at all times all that the Lord has spoken to you through His Word. In all areas of life, you are to apply the Word steadfastly in order to be able to possess your inheritance in God. Those who have undergone correction and change are always mindful not to sin against God anymore or go against His corrections concerning their lives.

To watch means to keep on looking up to Jesus as the author and finisher of your faith. Looking up to Him, He is where your help comes from. Once you have this mentality, you will surely make it in your Christian walk.

The Word of the Lord will continue to grow and produce fruit, making you a winner at all times.

Every one of us is expected to lead men back to God and His Kingdom through the Word of the Lord. Do not enter into any temptation or trial by your mistakes. Let him that has an ear to hear, let him listen to, perceive and understand what the Lord is saying to the churches, for it will benefit all who heed to this correction. They will overcome and inherit the promise.

God designed each and every one of us to bear fruit. He also desires that our fruit should remain and not be destroyed. The fruit of our changes are meant to bring more souls to the Kingdom of the Lord. Watch what you get involved in and choose to give attention to so that you don't go astray. Watch who you follow, where you go and how you mingle with people because darkness and light have nothing in common. A true child of God is not supposed to be involved in the things of darkness by any means.

That is why it is written in Romans 8:1: *Therefore now there is no condemnation to them that are in Christ Jesus who walk not after the flesh but after the spirit.*

Every believer who has believed God is not permitted to walk after the flesh anymore, but after the spirit. The Spirit will help you live above sin and temptation on daily basis. Whoever knows God does not live in the flesh. He is dead to the works of the flesh and the Spirit takes great control of his life to the extent that he no longer has a will of his own, but always does God's will.

Watch to see whether the Holy Spirit is still in control in your life and destiny. Watch to see whether you are still in faith with God. Watch to see whether you still keep the commandment of God. All these are yardsticks for measuring whether you can reach your peak in God. The days are evil and perilous. You must be watchful to be a good example that the upcoming generation can emulate. Our God is a good God and blessed is everyone whom He shall find doing His Word when He comes. Allow the things of God to take precedent of your life. Remember He said no weapon of the enemy formed against you shall prosper in any way. Watch and pray. Remember Jesus' watchword at the time of His testing. Jesus told the apostles, "Can you not watch with me an hour?"

Wait and be patient for after your obedience has been fulfilled, you will be ready to discipline all disobedience. There is nothing Lord cannot do in and through those who heed His warnings.

In Acts 20:9-12: *And there sat in a window a certain young man named Eutychus being fallen into a deep sleep, and as Paul was long preaching, he sunk down with sleep, and fell down from the third loft, and was taken up dead. And Paul went down and fell on him and embracing him said, trouble not yourselves, for his life is in him. When he therefore was come up again, and had broken bread, and eaten, and talked a long while, even till break of day, so he departed. And they brought the young man alive, and were not a little comforted.*

Now, Eutychus was fast asleep when other men around him were wide-eyed and watchful with every readiness to accomplish what was being preached. This caused his life to be shortened prematurely. If it were not for divine intervention through Paul, his destiny would have been truncated.

Many people do the same thing in their lives even today. Many good things going on in the world pass them by just because they were asleep when they ought to have been awake. The end is always death, if it were not for the mercies of God.

Paul ran down to him, embraced him and life returned again to him. This signifies God's merciful power and dominion. Let the world around you know that it is time to arise, and open our eyes to what God wants concerning your destiny. This is not the time to sleep away, but time to arise and shine for the light of the Lord has come upon us. It is time to thresh, for the harvest is ripe. You are the one to change your environment. It is not the environment that is supposed to change you.

Arise today and watch over the life and divine destiny the Lord has given you. Do not allow it to waste in any way. Try to put it in order and use it also to change another person's world. You are created to show forth the praise of God. Showing forth the praise of God means affecting another person's life with the good things God has done in your life. Watch out and affect your world with His goodness.

# CHAPTER EIGHT

# THE POWER TO CHANGE

*Therefore, now if any man be in Christ he is a new creature old thins are past away behold, all things are become new.*
(1 Cor. 5:17)

Corrections accepted bring about a definite change of life and destiny. Coming to the knowledge of the truth in God will make you a changed person, and once you change, your environment will also change; your relationships, your life with your loved ones, your language and thoughts will all begin to take on a new shape because of change.

Change is a one subject matter on earth that is in the mouth and mind of everyone. But change can never happen except a man makes it to happen. You must choose to change. Everything on earth will remain at a particular position until someone makes the conscience decision and effort to move it.

Change can never allow you to remain where you are. It can never be the same anymore because change has a power or force to cause a shift in destiny. If any man be in Christ, he is a new creature; old things are passed away, all things have become new. He is no longer in the old world.

Once you are in the know, you leave the realm of ignorance. Knowledge is power and life. A wise man scales the city of the mighty. Even when a man is not mighty but full of wisdom, he will achieve what the mighty cannot. He can do great exploits in all areas of life.

Change has the power to change others within its environment wherever it is found. This is why the Word says that light shines in darkness and the darkness comprehends it not. Light brings about change. The more light you have, the higher you fly in life. The power of change brings about promotion and increase. So change and become a world changer today. See you at the top!

# THE POWER OF CORRECTION APPENDIX

Summary and Scriptures Profitable for Correction

Job 38:1-7 & 2 Tim 3:16-17

Prov.29:17: *Correct your son and he will give you rest. Yes he will give delight to your soul.*

Prov.23:13 -14:2: *Do not withhold correction from a child for if you do beat him with a rod he will not die. You shall beat him with a rod and deliver his soul from hell.*

Psalm 39:11: *When with rebukes you correct man from iniquity*

Psalm 94:10: *He who instructs the nation's shall he not correct*

Jer. 2:19: *Own wickedness corrects me*

Heb 12:9: *Fathers corrected us*

Job 5:17: *Happy man God corrects*

Prov. 3:11 *But we not weary of his correction*

Prov. 3:12: *Whom the Lord loveth he corrects*

Prov. 22:15: *Rod of correction shall drive foolishness*

Hab. 1:12: *Established them for correction.*
Another Bible translation says: *You have marked them for correction.*

Prov.29:12: *He who is often rebuked and harden his neck will suddenly be destroyed and that without remedy.*

## What is Correction?

Correction is the rectification of defects or errors, misunderstandings, assumptions, misleading presentations and incorrect statements. To correct means to maintain accuracy.

2Tim. 3:16 -17: *A leader is to lay the foundation, providing directory confront others when they err, correct their behaviour and help them to progress again*

## The Power of Correction

If I cannot correct you, I am in error. And if you cannot receive my correction, you are also in error. The inability to receive correction is scriptural deviation and the ability to receive correction reveals your inner character and your desire for growth. It communicates who you truly are.

The requirements for a Christian are:

> To have a humble spirit
> To have a teachable spirit
> To be accountable
> To be a fervent servant
> To be obedient
> To bow to authority
> To display maturity
> To be willing to learn.

This can be interpreted in two ways:

- Doing what you are asked to do equals availability.

- Not doing what you are asked to do or doing what you are asked to do in your own way also mean unavailable.

There is such a thing as the Instructional Self, which means being the instructor and the instructee by following your own way, will and thoughts.

Define your co-operation, co-existence within the unity of fellow Christians and highlights your skills, if any, as a team worker and a valuable team member reveals your cooperation with the kingdom vision.

It reveals your understanding of value and principle within the organisation. What you value ,you protect. You cannot, and do not wish, to run it down, but build it up (Prov.14:1 & Prov.13:1).

## Correction is the Oil of Love (Prov. 3:12)

If you cannot be corrected:

1. It means you are not ready to serve and that you do not have the heart of a servant, rather you are selfish, arrogant and prideful. Correction works through love; it always takes love to correct. Anyone who refuses to correct others in error is an enemy. It is only those that hate you that will not correct because they want your failure and downfall.

   Correction is an act of loving; it is also for our protection, prevention, preservation and promotion.

2. Correction does not harm and does not disrespect. Its unique motive is to help and enhance your performance and value.

3. It is disloyal not to take correction from your boss. It also displays a lack of common sense or spiritual wisdom not to listen to the advice of your staff.

You cannot correct your boss but you can advise him/her with a spirit of submission and a respectful attitude. Moreover, you can only advise your boss if you have built a good reputation in the organisation through good character reference, using the following checklist:

- Good attitude towards work, staff and co-workers
- Record of hard work and no display of laziness
- Punctuality
- High productivity levels
- A team work spirit or attitude
- Discipline
- Time keeping (this is covered in punctuality)
- Good reports
- Good example
- High commitment level
- High level of obedience
- Good customer service (promotes core values and good relationship skills)
- Effective communication skills; wise and calm in dealing with others, firm, accurate, clear and solution oriented

# The Benefits of Correction

- It corrects the defects
- It improves services
- It builds strong foundations that are impeccable and accurate
- It improves relationships and encourages better understanding
- It helps to maintain focus and avoid distractions
- It helps to eliminate errors and biblical deviations
- It helps to promote value and excellence
- It helps to improve performance, growth and development
- It helps to build up self-esteem and confidence
- It provides empowerment for greater authority
- It helps to avoid immaturity
- It helps to eliminate shame and disgrace
- It protects your image and defines your values

# The Power of Correction

Correction is the implementation of discipline and creative order, scriptural order, behavioural order, physical order or spiritual order that initiates progress.

Correction can effect change and correct defects, for good value and better standards. The instrument of correction is the Word of God.

Heb. 12:5-11, 2Tim. 2:20 -24, 2Tim. 4:1-5.

www.ingramcontent.com/pod-product-compliance
Lightning Source LLC
Chambersburg PA
CBHW071035080526
44587CB00015B/2621